BAAL SHEM TOV

RABBI YISRAEL BEN ELIEZER

VOLUME II

DIVINE LIGHT

MYSTICAL WISDOM OF THE

LEGENDARY KABBALAH MASTER

Compiled and Freely Adapted

by **Tzvi Meir Cohn**

BST Publishing
Cleveland, Ohio

First Printing 2009

Collection, adaptation, introductory material by Howard Cohn

Translation by Rabbi Doctor Eliezer Shore

Copyright©2009 by Tzvi Meir (Howard Martin) Cohn

Cover Design by Aitan Levy

Cover art by Beena Sklare

Printed in the United States of America

For information regarding permission to reprint material from this book, please e-mail your request to BST Publishing, Permissions Department at info@bstpublishing.com.

ISBN: 978-0-9792865-0-6

Library of Congress Control Number: 2009901726

Library of Congress subject heading:

1. Hasidim — Legends. 2. Baal Shem Tov, ca. 1698-1760 — Legends. 3. Hasidism. 4. Mysticism Judaism. 5. Title.

BST Publishing
Cleveland, OH 44122
info@bstpublishing.com
www.bstpublishing.com

יברכך יי וישמרך

יאר יי פניו אליך ויחנך

ישא יי פניו אליך וישם לך שלום

"May the L•rd bless you and guard you. May
the L•rd make His countenance shine upon
you and be gracious to you. May the L•rd
turn His countenance towards you and grant
you peace."[1]

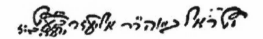

Yisrael Ben Moreinu Rabbeinu HaRav Rav Eliezer
KoesB (presently in) Mezibush
Signature of the Baal Shem Tov

---

[1] Numbers 6:24-26

CONTENTS

INTRODUCTION

Although each of the stories or anecdotes in this collection has been printed in other collections of Chassidic stories and teachings, they were all originally transmitted as an oral tradition. They have each been **FREELY ADAPTED** and published by me for the purpose of hastening the coming of Moshiach.[1]

Throughout this collection I used the Ashkenazi (Eastern European) pronunciation of the Hebrew rather than the Sephardic pronunciation used in Israel. The reason is that the anecdotes and teachings were originally told in Yiddish[2] with the Ashkenazi pronunciation of the Hebrew and I want you to get the flavor as well as the teachings of the stories and anecdotes. For example, Shabbat is presented as Shabbos and Mitzvot is written as Mitzvos.

Another point to understand is that the Hebrew word "reb" refers to the position of the

---

[1] The word "Messiah" comes from the Hebrew word Moshiach meaning "the anointed one."
[2] Jewish

man concerned. It is used immediately before a proper name and never as an independent word.

When speaking of the chassidic saints we use the title "Rebbe," but in speaking about them we use the shorter title 'Reb.' Rebbe signifies a somewhat higher degree of worthiness. There are some saints whose greatness is such that neither title is appropriate. In this case, we give them both titles together — Rebbe Reb. There are only a few such saints. Among them are Rebbe Reb Dov Ber (the Maggid), Rebbe Reb Shmelke of Mikulov and his brother Rebbe Reb Elimelech of Lizensk, and Rebbe Reb Zusha of Annipol.

I would like to express my gratitude to many people who have made this book possible.

Rabbi Sholom Ber Chaikin for reading the manuscript of this book, checking for errors and catching various mistakes of fact and occasionally tone.

Rabbi Michoel Feinstein for editing the manuscript of this book.

Aitan HaLevi Levy, whose creativity and contributions have been invaluable for bringing this book to publication.

Robert Burruss, my friend, for your insights and help.

My sons, Daniel Menachem Mendel HaCohane and Avraham Schneur Zalman HaCohane, for being the bright lights of my life.

May G•d, blessed be He, shower blessings on all those who have helped in the preparation of this book.

Most importantly, my deepest appreciation and thanks to my dearest wife Basha, whose constant support, assistance, encouragement and love provided the very foundation of this sefer.

Of course, none of this would be possible without Ha Kodosh Boruch Hu,[1] whom I thank "exceedingly with my mouth; amid the many I will praise Him."[2]

---

[1] The Holy One, Blessed be He
[2] Psalms 109:30

FOREWORD

INTO the terrifying, dark night that marked Jewish life in seventeenth and eighteenth century Eastern Europe, Heaven sent Rabbi Yisrael ben Eliezer, otherwise known as the Baal Shem Tov. His mission was to reveal to the masses of ordinary, unlearned Jewish people their immense spiritual value and to strengthen their dedication to live according to their ancestral heritage, that of the path of Torah and Mitzvos. He accomplished his mission by founding the Chassidic movement and spreading the new teachings of Chassidus.

The basis of Chassidic thought derives from the powerful spirit of the Baal Shem Tov probing the mystical aspects of the Torah. The most fundamental teaching of Chassidism is the omnipresence of G•d, that the whole universe is a manifestation of the Divine. This manifestation is not an emanation but an actual portion of G•d; nothing is separate from G•d. Therefore, everything in creation, including man, animals, plants and even inanimate objects are directly and at all times overseen by G•d.

Characterized by his extraordinary sincerity and humility, the Baal Shem Tov spoke directly to the masses of unlearned Jews. His teachings emphasized each person's continuous spiritual union with G•d and that enthusiasm and joy are essential to an experiential relationship with the Holy One, blessed be He.

Chassidus was cherished and loved by the common and often illiterate Jews. Among them, it found its home. Chassidic sayings of wisdom and stories about the leaders of the various Chassidic communities became part of a vibrant way of life that thrives until today.

The beis midrash[1] of the holy Baal Shem Tov served as a synagogue and as a place to gather and learn Torah. Moreover, it became a spiritual center that drew his followers and even non-believers for advice and blessings.

---

[1] Study hall

The Baal Shem Tov instilled his very spirit into his inner circle of followers, known as the "Chevraya Kadisha."[1] His teachings struck a responsive chord in their hearts, and they eagerly undertook to follow his way of worship and thought. These devout followers saw in the Baal Shem Tov the image of the ancient ideal — a master of Torah who embodied the personal power of King David and the spiritual countenance of an angel. Thus, they considered it a rare privilege to spend time in the presence of their Rebbe.

Those of the inner circle were the first sources that absorbed the miraculous stories and accounts of the Baal Shem Tov. Often, they were eye witnesses to the miraculous deeds themselves, or they heard of the miracles directly from those who were involved. Thus, the wondrous tales of the Baal Shem Tov took form as oral narrative and spread from them

---

[1] Holy Fellowship

among the masses of the Jewish people, echoing the world over.

The deeds and sayings of the Baal Shem Tov tell their own story; they speak for themselves. There is no need for explanations and interpretations. A pure heart and a Divine soul will certainly be moved by the actions and sayings of one who devoted his entire life to lead, guide and inspire Jewish people to live a life filled with joy and in accordance with their ancestral Torah traditions.

The purpose of this book is to shine the Baal Shem Tov's Divine light upon those drawn to its contents.

PART I

THE SOUL OF THE

BAAL SHEM TOV

A soul like that of the Baal Shem Tov comes into this world but once in a thousand years.[1]

[1] In name of Rabbi Yisrael of Koshnitz (1740-1814), a disciple of the Maggid of Mezritch

THE soul of the Baal Shem Tov was so lofty that it would have been impossible for it to enter this world if his father had experienced any physical desire.[1] Therefore, his father was one hundred years old when the Baal Shem Tov was born. His desires had already abated, and the Baal Shem Tov was only conceived with G•d's help.[2]

[1] There is a classic teaching, stretching as far back as the Midrash, that the thoughts of the parents during marital relations affect the nature of the children who are born. The soul of the Baal Shem Tov so transcended physicality that he could only be born to elderly parents, individuals who no longer had physical desires. Rashis Chochmah, Shaar HaKedusha Ch. 17

[2] *Imrei Noam*

THE Zohar says, "If a person is worthy, Heaven gives him the nefesh-soul. If he is more worthy, Heaven gives him the ruach-soul. If he is even more worthy, Heaven gives him the neshama-soul. If he is still more worthy, Heaven gives him the neshama to the neshama-soul."[1] Rabbi Mordechai of Chernobyl[2] said that the Baal Shem Tov's soul was from this highest of levels, the neshama to the neshama-soul.

It is known that the nefesh-soul comes from the spiritual world of Asiyah (Action), the ruach-soul from the spiritual world of Yetzirah (Formation), the neshama-soul from the spiritual world of Beriyah (Creation), and the neshama to the neshama-soul from the spiritual world of Atzilus (Emanation). The soul of Baal Shem Tov was from the spiritual world of Atzilus.[3]

∞

---

[1] Zohar 2:94b
[2] 1770—1837
[3] *Tzror HaChaim* in the name of the Trisker Rav

PART II

THE GREATNESS OF
THE BAAL SHEM TOV

BEFORE the Baal Shem Tov was born, there were terrible decrees against the Jews, such as the massacres by the anti-Semitic Ukranian barbarians, Chmielnicki and his army in 1648 and 1649.[1] The situation of the Jews throughout Europe was dire, both spiritually and economically. The landlords harassed them, the priests falsely accused them of crimes they had not committed and not a year passed in which the Jews did not suffer from these libels, physically, spiritually and financially.

The economic and living conditions of the Jews fell to such as low level that their spiritual state was so seriously affected that they entered a state of spiritual slumber and unconsciousness.

In Heaven, they saw that in order to arouse the Jews and elevate them, both materially and spiritually, a uniquely superior soul must descend to the world; the soul of our teacher the Baal Shem Tov, who is named,

---

[1] Estimated 100,00 to 200,00 Jews killed in what was considered first pogrom

"Yisrael," after the nation of Israel. The tried and trusted way to revive someone who has fainted is to call him by his name. For this reason, the soul of Yisrael Baal Shem Tov descended to this world to awake the nation of Israel from their spiritual slumber.[1]

[1] *Likuti Sichos* Vol. 2 P. 516 Quoting the Maamar of the Rebbe Rashab 5663 P.251

THE Holy Rabbi Moshe of Kobrin[1] said, "We must believe all the stories, miracles, and wonders attributed to the Baal Shem Tov. We should believe that even if they didn't happen, they could have happened."[2]

---

[1] 1784—1858
[2] *Imros Tahoros*, p. 34

THE author of Toldos Yitzchak, Rabbi Yitzchak of Neshchiz,[1] said in the name of his father that not all of the miracle stories told about Tzaddikim[2] are authentic, for many seem implausible. Not so with the stories of the Baal Shem Tov because even if the miracle attributed to him didn't actually happen, the Baal Shem Tov could have done it.[3]

---

[1] Rabbi Yitzchak Isaac Weisz (1824—1894)
[2] Saintly, righteous individuals
[3] *Zichron Tov*, p. 9b

IF a person were to come and tell me, "I saw the Baal Shem Tov build a ladder and climb to heaven alive, physically, in his clothing," I would believe him, for whatever they say about the Baal Shem Tov is possible.[1]

---

[1] The Seer of Lublin, Rabbi Yaakov Yitzchak of Lublin (1745–1815)

THE Tzaddik Reb Leib Sarah's[1] once sat with a saintly friend of his and exchanged stories about different Tzaddikim. As soon as they began talking about the Baal Shem Tov, Reb Leib Sarah's body started trembling.

"You speak of this great Tanah![2] I will tell you what he was. Had he lived in the times of the Gaonim,[3] he would have been a Gaon. In the generation of the Amoraim,[4] he would have been an Amora, and in the era of the Prophets[5] he would have been a prophet. Had he lived in time of our Forefathers[6] he would have been a significant figure. What do I mean by this? Just as we say 'The G•d of Abraham, Isaac and Jacob,' so would we have said 'The G•d of Yisrael.'"[7]

∞

---

[1] 1730—1796
[2] Rabbinic Sages 70 CE to 200 CE
[3] Title given to the heads of the Jewish academies at Sura and Pumbedita in Babylonia from seventh century until the middle of the 11th century.
[4] 220 CE to 500 CE
[5] 1050 BCE to 450 BCE
[6] Abraham, Isaac and Jacob
[7] *Siach Sarfei Kodesh*

THE Baal Shem Tov was initially incapable of speaking with ordinary people because of his devekus.[1] Later, his Heavenly mentor, Achiyah HaShaloni,[2] taught him to recite certain psalms which enabled him to speak plainly without losing his concentration.[3]

---

[1] An intense attachment to Heaven
[2] In prior incarnations, Achiyah HaShaloni witnessed the exodus from Egypt, was a prophet during the time of King David, and taught Elijah the Prophet.
[3] *Shivchei Baal Shem Tov*

THE Holy Rabbi of Ruzhin[1] said that although many people claim that the Baal Shem Tov earned his name because he used holy names,[2] this was not so. Rather, "the Tzaddik rules with the fear of G•d,"[3] for "G•d decrees and the Tzaddik annuls."[4] He was called the Baal Shem Tov because he annulled many decrees issued by Heaven against the Jewish people.[5] [6]

---

[1] Rabbi Yisrael Friedman (1797—1850)
[2] "Baal Shem Tov" literally means, "Master of the Good Name." The Baal Shem Tov used these holy names for contemplative and healing purposes.
[3] II Samuel 23:3
[4] Mo'ed Katan 16b
[5] In other words, "Master of the Good Name" – Baal Shem Tov – means "Master of HaShem (G•d)," for the Tzaddik has the power to annul heavenly decrees.
[6] *Yeshuos Yisroel*, 2:6

A great Tzaddik who knows how to perform unifications and combinations of Divine Names can rectify what is wrong with a person just by looking at them. Through these unifications, the Tzaddik immediately causes the person to have thoughts of repentance. The Baal Shem Tov said that he could fix a person instantly by merely looking at them. But if the person stubbornly refused to repent, the Baal Shem Tov would completely remove the holy spark that needed repair from within them.[1]

---

[1] *Toldos Aharon*, Vayera

"**I** heard that a certain reincarnated soul came to the Baal Shem Tov for a tikkun.[1] The soul had had belonged to a great man who had lived in the time of the Arizal.[2] The soul had not been permitted by Heaven to go to the Tzaddikim of previous generations and had been waiting several centuries for the Baal Shem Tov, so that it could be repaired."[3]

---

[1] Spiritual repair

[2] Arizal — acronym for Eloki Rabbi Yitzchak — the Divinely inspired Rabbi Yitzchak Luria (1535 — 1572) — whose teachings became central for virtually all Kabbalistic thought thereafter

[3] Rabbi Shlomo HaKohen of Radamsk author of *Tiferes Shlomo*, Shabbos Chanukah

THE Baal Shem Tov was an incomparable Torah giant, involved in Torah study throughout his life. He had no equal. His saintly student, Reb Yaakov Yosef HaKohane of Polonoye, the author of Toldos Yaakov Yoseph,[1] said that before his departure from this world he would ask G•d to credit him for all the Torah and mitzvos of his entire life with the same value He gave to the Baal Shem Tov's heavenly thoughts when the latter smoked his pipe.[2]

---

[1] The first printed Chassidic book, published in 1780
[2] *Zohar Cha-Truma*

ONE day, Reb Dovid,[1] head of the Ostrow Beis Din, was shown by the Baal Shem Tov the new heavens that he had created by his thoughts while smoking. Reb Dovid fell into a faint from the awe and fear that the sight inspired in him. The Baal Shem Tov was worthy of all this through constant study of Torah for its own sake, through prayer with a minyan,[2] and through daily purification in a mikveh.[3] [4]

---

[1] d. 1750
[2] A quorum of ten men required for certain religious obligations
[3] Pool of water for spiritual immersion
[4] *Zohar Chai-Truma*

PART III

EXPERIENCING THE

BAAL SHEM TOV

WHEN the Baal Shem Tov would study Torah with his students, they would be surrounded by fire and the ministering angels would gather around them. They would hear the voices and thunder heard by the Children of Israel during the giving of the Torah at Mount Sinai, and the words "I am the L•rd your G•d," from the mouth of G•d.[1]

---

[1] *Heichal HaBracha* Va'eschanan

THE Maggid of Mezritch,[1] successor to the Baal Shem Tov, was once asked for a favor by his disciple and successor, Reb Schneur Zalman,[2] later known as the Alter Rebbe.

"Ask what you will," the Maggid said.

"I wish to know the essence of the Baal Shem Tov," replied Reb Schneur Zalman.

"You have asked a difficult question," the Maggid answered. "Had he lived during the era of the Tannaim[3], he would have been remarkable; had he lived in the period of the Prophets he would have been an innovation, while in the times of our Forefathers he would also have been significant."

This anecdote was related by the Tzemach Tzedek.[4] He went on to add that his grandfather, Rabbi Schneur Zalman, had continued, "If I had not heard this directly from my Rebbe (the Mezritcher Maggid), who knew

---

[1] Rebbe Reb Dov Ber (1710—1772), the successor to the Baal Shem Tov
[2] Founder of the Chabad Chassidic dynasty (1745—1812)
[3] Rabbinic Sages (700CE—2000CE)
[4] Rabbi Menachem Mendel Schneerson (1789—1866), the grandson of the Alter Rebbe and the third Rebbe of Chabad

the Baal Shem Tov from personal observation
and experience, I would not have believed that
the Baal Shem Tov had been born of a woman."[1]

---

[1] *Sipurei Baal Shem Tov*

IT is known that the Mezritcher Maggid thought that the Baal Shem Tov ate as an angel until one time he actually saw him eat as ordinary people do.[1]

[1] *Or Hachochmo*, Parshas Beshalach

THE following story was told many times by the Alter Rebbe, who heard it from his Rebbe, the Mezritcher Maggid.

Once, the Baal Shem Tov was teaching the Chevraya Kadisha unfathomable secrets of the Torah that had never before been heard in this world. These secrets could not even be found in any of the writings of the early mekubolim[1] or even the Arizal.

All the Baal Shem Tov's disciples were Torah giants in their own right, especially the eminent Reb Dov Ber. Even before coming to the Baal Shem Tov, Reb Dov Ber was famous for having studied and reviewed every available book of Torah, both of revealed knowledge and mystical thought, one hundred and one times.

Upon this occasion, Reb Dov Ber heard previously unknown teachings about such deep concepts of Torah that they utterly confused him. As he thought about the Baal Shem Tov's ability to transmit such teachings, he found it

---

[1] Masters of Kabbalah

difficult to believe that a soul enclothed in flesh and blood could know such hidden knowledge, probably beyond even the grasp of the angels themselves. He was seized with the thought that the voice that spoke from the mouth of the Baal Shem Tov came directly from his disembodied soul.

At the same time, several of the other disciples were so mesmerized by these teachings that they finally were compelled to touch the Baal Shem's hand to see if it was tangible.[1]

---

[1] *Niflaos Sipurim*

ONCE, the Baal Shem Tov was outside the city of Mezibush with his students, and the time for Mincha[1] arrived. His disciples said to him, "Rebbe, there is no water to wash our hands for Mincha." The Baal Shem Tov took his walking stick and struck the earth and a spring of water burst from the ground. It flows until today, near Mezibush, and is called the Baal Shem Tov's well.

The Baal Shem Tov did many miraculous acts, the likes of which had not been seen since the days of the Tannaim,[2] Rabbi Shimon bar Yochai[3] and Rabbi Chanina ben Dosa.[4] All the miracles were as a result of his constant attachment to G•d.[5]

∞

---

[1] The afternoon prayer service
[2] Rabbinic Sages (700 CE—2000 CE)
[3] Author of Zohar
[4] 1ˢᵗ century
[5] *Notzer Chesed, Chap. 6*

WHEN the Baal Shem Tov first took up residence in Mezibush, several of the local rabbis opposed his teachings and his way of practicing Judaism. These rabbis visited him during the holiday of Succos and told him that his succah was not built in accordance with Torah law. The Baal Shem Tov argued unsuccessfully that his succah was kosher. Then, he rested his head in his hands for a few moments. When he lifted his head and opened his hands, he held a piece of parchment. On the parchment was written, "The succah of Rabbi Yisrael Baal Shem Tov is kosher. Thus says Matat,[1] the Prince of the Countenance."

That parchment was inherited by the Baal Shem Tov's grandson, the holy Rabbi Moshe Chaim Ephraim of Sudilkov.[2] Whenever someone became ill, he would tell the family to

---

[1] Matat is one of the most important angels in the heavenly hierarchy. He is a member of a special group that is permitted to look at G•d's countenance, an honor most angels do not share.
[2] The author of Degel Machane Ephraim (1740—1799)

place the parchment under the sick person's head. The person would immediately recover.

This practice continued for two years. The parchment was put under the pillow of every sick person and he or she would immediately get better. During the entire two-year period, not one person in the city of Sudilkov passed away.

One day, the parchment was put under the head of a sick person, and it disappeared. Reb Moshe Chaim explained that it had been revealed to him that Heaven was not pleased with what he was doing, for all those born must eventually die. Therefore, he had prayed that the parchment be taken back by Heaven.

I heard from honest people who heard directly from the Tzaddik Reb Yoskie, the grandson of Rabbi Moshe Chaim Ephraim, that he personally saw the parchment in his grandfather's possession.[1]

---

[1] *From a Letter of the Rabbi of Mezibush*

AND then there was the time that several of the Baal Shem Tov's students entered his study at the same time. He spoke to them, advising each about his particular problem. When the group left the study, they discussed what the Baal Shem Tov had told each one separately. They were stunned to discover that at the time they had all stood together in the study, each had been positive that the Baal Shem Tov had addressed him alone. To their amazement, they found that he had spoken to each one about his individual problem without the others being aware of what was said to his neighbor.[1]

---

[1] *Emunas Tzaddikim*

RABBI Yitzchak Isaac of Komarno[1] said that my teacher and father-in-law, Rabbi Avraham Mordechai of Finshtov, had told him that one of the disciples of the Baal Shem Tov asked the Rebbe, "What will be my livelihood?"

The Baal Shem Tov responded, "You will be a cantor."

The surprised disciple exclaimed, "But Rebbe, I can't sing!"

The Baal Shem Tov replied, "I will bind you to the World of Melody."

The man became the greatest cantor in the world. Once, this cantor came to Rebbe Reb Elimelech of Lizensk.[2] An intense discussion ensued between the Rebbe and his son, the Tzaddik Reb Elazar, over whether or not to honor the cantor with leading the Kabbalas Shabbos[3] service. Reb Elimelech was afraid that the cantor would disrupt him from the state of

---

[1] 1766—1834
[2] A disciple of the Maggid of Mezritch (1717—1787)
[3] Prayer service beginning Shabbos evening prayers

holiness he normally experienced during the Shabbos prayers.

Finally, they decided to honor the cantor and his two accompanists with leading the Kabbalas Shabbos service. Their decision was a result of their great awe of the Baal Shem Tov, for the cantor was known as "the Cantor of the Baal Shem Tov." Out of respect for the Baal Shem Tov, they decided to honor him, and whatever would be, would be.

When the cantor and his two accompanists began to sing the prayers to welcome Shabbos, Reb Elimelech sent word that the second accompanist should stop singing, and only the cantor and the remaining accompanist should continue. Afterward, he ordered even the cantor and accompanist to stop, for he was afraid that he would be annihilated in the Divine light emanating from their singing.

"On subsequent Shabbosim, Reb Elimelech showed honor to the cantor, but because of his fear, he would not allow him to pray before the congregation."[1]

∞

---

[1] *From the Manuscripts of Rabbi Yitzchak Isaac of Komarno*

AFTER Shabbos, Reb Elimelech asked the cantor to tell him about the holiness of the Baal Shem Tov. The cantor told him about awesome things that no one had heard before.

Primarily, he spoke of the Baal Shem Tov's love and awe of G•d, and how he would perform soul ascensions to the spiritual worlds while fully conscious in this world. He would gaze into all the chambers of Torah and see the Divine Chariot. When the Baal Shem Tov would recite Hallel, he would not say a verse until he saw the angels who recited that particular verse and heard the exquisiteness of their song, and could recite the verse with them.

He related the awe-inspiring holiness of the Baal Shem Tov from the day of his birth. He described how he would speak to the souls of Tzaddikim, with Elijah the Prophet, and most often with the Arizal, who was constantly with him.

Once, the cantor related, the Baal Shem Tov asked the Arizal why he had openly taught mystical secrets of the Torah outside of the context of worship. The Arizal answered that if he had lived another two years, he would have taught the mystical secrets of the Torah in the context of prayer so that the G•dly sparks, still lost in the world would have been rectified.

The cantor spoke about how the Baal Shem Tov's soul ascensions occurred while his body lay still, and how the Baal Shem Tov would speak to Moshiach[1] and with our teacher Moses.

He talked about how the Baal Shem Tov was an expert in the "Work of Creation,"[2] the "Work of the Chariot,"[3] and in the entire Torah. He described how the Baal Shem Tov spoke the language of every creature and the language of the angels, and how he was filled with love and awe of G•d and all possible virtues of character, including piety, humility, and love of Israel.

Reb Elimelech commented that all the spiritual attainments attributed to the Arizal also applied to the Baal Shem Tov — perhaps

---

[1] Messiah — Direct descendant of King David — King and Ruler of the Jewish people during the Messianic Age
[2] Kabbalistic doctrine
[3] Kabbalistic doctrine

even more so. He further said that that which is written about the Arizal is a drop in the ocean compared with the totality of who the Arizal really was.

The cantor also told Reb Elimelech that every Friday afternoon, during the Mincha prayer, tens of thousands of souls would gather around the Baal Shem Tov, and he would spiritually heal their soul and help them return to their source.[1]

[1] *From the Manuscripts of Rabbi Yitzchak Isaac of Komarno*

ON another occasion, the cantor told Reb Elimelech that when the Baal Shem Tov would look at any object, such as a bench or a table, he could tell all the thoughts that the craftsman had when he made that object. Reb Elimelech was astounded by this.

Later in the conversation, the cantor told Reb Elimelech how the Baal Shem Tov could gaze from one end of the earth to the other.

Once, when his students were sitting with him, the Baal Shem Tov chuckled a little, as he often did. His students asked him why he chuckled. He said that in a certain city, in a very distant land, a nobleman had spent several years building a beautiful palace. And just a few minutes before, a Tzaddik had been on his way to the synagogue to pray. It had started to hail heavily, so the Tzaddik took shelter in the palace that the nobleman had spent so long building.

When the hail storm stopped, the Tzaddik left the palace and continued on to the synagogue. As soon as he left, the palace collapsed.

"How can I not laugh over how much G•d's direction of the world is hidden? The purpose of this great building was to give shelter to this Tzaddik for a short while. During that time, the Tzaddik rectified all of the sparks of holiness that were in the stones which formed the sides of the palace. Once the sparks were rectified, the stones no longer needed to remain standing. That is why the palace immediately collapsed."

Later, the cantor continued, we saw in the newspaper the story of that palace and its unexplained collapse. It had happened at the moment that the Baal Shem Tov had laughed.

Then, the cantor stood up and swore that once, while he and the other students studied Torah with the Baal Shem Tov, flames had risen around them. The flames remained until they were so purified that they heard the Torah from the Rebbe as the Children of Israel had received it at Mount Sinai — with thunder and lightening and the mighty blasts of the shofar! In fact, the cantor went on to say that because the sounds at Mount Sinai were Divine and never ceased. However, a person needed holiness and purity to hear them.

Reb Elimelech replied, "I have not achieved that spiritual level. Though it comes as no surprise, that the spiritual service and holiness of our Master and Rebbe, Rabbi Yisrael Baal Shem Tov was extremely great. Moreover, his holy practices were from that pure place, the Nestur River, and from Achiya HaShiloni. Fortunate is the person who merits that state."

The G•d-fearing who read this will understand that all the above-mentioned levels, or similar ones, were attained by Reb Elimelech.[1]

---

[1] *From the Manuscripts of Rabbi Yitzchak Isaac of Komarno*

SOMETIME later, the Baal Shem Tov's cantor passed away. One Friday afternoon, within the Shloshim,[1] his bass accompanist returned to his home after immersing in the mikvah.

"Hurry!" he said to his wife. "Call the burial society and prepare! In Heaven, they are honoring my cantor to greet the Sabbath but he refuses to do so without me." Then the bass accompanist lay down on his bed and left this world.[2]

[1] First thirty days of mourning
[2] *From the Manuscripts of Rabbi Yitzchak Isaac of Komarno*

REB Yitzchak of Skver related that one Simchas Torah evening, the Baal Shem Tov was dancing among his Chassidim with a Sefer Torah in his arms. He gave the sacred scroll to one of his disciples to hold as he danced alone.

Another disciple, Reb Isaac, saw this and remarked, "Our holy Rebbe gave the tangible scroll away while he himself kept the spiritual scroll."

The Baal Shem Tov heard this and exclaimed, "I am surprised that Reb Isaac was able to observe and understand this!"[1]

---

[1] *Sipurei Baal Shem Tov*

THE Tzaddik, Rabbi Yosef of Yampeleh, the son of Reb Yechiel Michel of Zlotchov,[1] prayed with intense concentration, especially during the evening prayer. Such was his intensity that he was critical of anyone who did not pray this way. His holy father, Reb Michel, once said of him, "My son Yosef is able to pray."

Once, Rabbi Yosef became sick and fell into a coma. His soul ascended Above and was immersed in the Dinur River.[2] Afterwards, he was standing before the Heavenly Court. They were weighing all of his merits. All the prayers he had ever recited, from his childhood to the moment of his illness, were brought forth. Not one was missing.

Suddenly, a fearsome angel stepped forward and declared, "What, are these prayers!?" The angel blew upon them, and the prayers scattered, until nothing was left but the single Hebrew letter "hey." It shone with a pure

[1] Disciple of the Baal Shem Tov (1721–1786)
[2] The Dinur is a river of fire, in which souls must be immersed before being admitted to heaven.

light. Reb Yosef stood before the Heavenly Court so frightened that his hands were shaking.

On that same day, Reb Yosef's father, Reb Michel, unexpectedly passed away during the third meal of Shabbos. For the past two years, Reb Michel's family had carefully watched over him during that time of Shabbos. They feared that Reb Michel's soul would leave his body because of his intense attachment to G•d.

Ordinarily, Reb Michel ate the third Shabbos meal with some of his sons in his private quarters. Then he would go to the study hall to speak words of Torah and to sing with his Chassidim until the third Shabbos meal was over. Then he would return to his private study and pace back and forth in deep devekus. Reb Michel would repeatedly utter the words, "In that time of will, Moses departed"[1] until his face face burned like a fire.

_____

[1] The Zohar states that Moses died at the time of mincha on Shabbos. Shabbos mincha is the highest point of the week, the time when the inner will of G•d (ra'ava d'ra'avin) is revealed.

Once, at such a time, Reb Yosef of Zemigrad, a devout follower of Reb Michel, asked his brother the Tzaddik Rabbi Avraham Mordechai, "Do you see how the heels of our Reb Michel are standing in the Upper Garden of Eden?" Thus, it is understood why Reb Michel required special supervision.

On the occasion of his soul's passing, however, no one had been there for him. He had paced quickly back and forth in his room saying, "In that time of will, Moses departed." Just then his daughter looked in upon him. She rushed to tell her brother, Reb Yitzchak. He ran into the room and grabbed his father in an attempt to disrupt his thoughts and bring him out from his devekus. But to no avail. Reb Michel fell on his son's shoulder and cried, "Shema Yisrael, Hashem Elokeinu, Hashem Echad."[1] With those words, he departed this world.

---

[1] Hear O Israel, the L•rd is One the L•rd is G•d.

Meanwhile, Reb Yosef was still standing before the Heavenly Court, where he remained until Sunday morning. It was then that he heard a proclamation that all the Tzaddikim should go to welcome his father, Rabbi Yechiel Michel of Zlotchov, who had just arrived. All the Tzaddikim went. Among them was our Master, the Baal Shem Tov, who had been Reb Michel's teacher.

When Reb Michel saw his son Reb Yosef standing before the Heavenly Court, he cried, "Yosef, my son, what are you doing here?" Reb Yosef told him what had occurred. Without saying more, Reb Michel just left his son and continued to his place in Heaven.

Then, the Baal Shem Tov arrived. He quickly understood what was being debated by the Heavenly Court. Without hesitation, he stepped before the Court and said, "How can you claim that the prayers of my dear friend, Reb Yosef, are not pure? I will ask him to pray the evening prayer, and you will see that his prayers are indeed sincere and true."

The Baal Shem Tov called to Reb Yosef and said, "Pray here my son, before the Creator of all, and He will save you."

Reb Yosef began to pray, and with this one prayer, he lifted up all his other prayers, so that they all shone brightly.

Because of the great intensity with which he prayed, his physical body that was still below began to sweat profusely. He awoke and found he had been healed of his sickness. His mother and sisters were there caring for him. He said to them, "Remove your jewelry![1] Our father has passed away."[2] [3]

---

[1] As a sign of mourning, one must remove jewelry and make-up upon the death of a close relative.
[2] Perhaps Reb Yosef returned to consciousness at another location than the town where his father had died. Thus, his mother and sister might not have yet learned of their husband and father's passing. Another possibility is that his mother and sister may have been so busy crying for Reb Yosef, that they had forgotten to remove their jewelry, even though they were in mourning.
[3] *Nesiv Mitzvosecha: Nesiv Emunah, Shevil 3:25*

REBBE Reb Dov Ber of Mezritch did not want to attach himself to the Baal Shem Tov or to even go to see him. Only because of his extremely poor health, did he eventually seek the Baal Shem Tov's help and treatment.

At first, Reb Dov Ber was not impressed with the Baal Shem Tov. So the Baal Shem Tov had to show Reb Dov Ber miracles, in order to draw him under his influence.

The Baal Shem Tov asked Reb Dov Ber to join him in his study. There, the Baal Shem Tov read a few passages from Etz Chaim, a book of Kabbalah, and the Angels relating to each passage flew around the room while he was reading. That was enough to cause Reb Dov Ber to become his follower.

As it happened, the Baal Shem Tov brought about Reb Dov Ber's partial recovery from his poor health through prayers, supplications, and miracles.

The Baal Shem Tov even transmitted to Reb Dov Ber the ability to reach the source of all his wisdom. In this way, Reb Dov Ber could become the leader of the next generation.

The Divine light of Reb Dov Ber's holiness still shines through his disciples, from generation to generation. From their words we live, until the coming of Moshiach, may it be soon in our days.[1]

---

[1] *Tiferes Shlomo, Rimzei Purim.*

WHEN Reb Dov Ber first wanted to take leave of the Baal Shem Tov, the latter objected. In fact, the Baal Shem Tov repeatedly prevented Reb Dov Ber from going. Reb Dov Ber asked the Baal Shem Tov why he did not want him to leave. The Baal Shem Tov explained that his own mind was like a flowing spring — and the more water drawn from a flowing spring, the more strongly it flows.[1] [2]

---

[1] The Degel Machane Ephraim (Rabbi Moshe Ephriam of Sudlikov, 1740—1800), a great grandson of the Baal Shem Tov, writes that "In relation to his friends who heed him and who are like students, each person is a fountain of wisdom that flows ever-stronger — the more his students draw from him, the more robust the fountain's flow. As long as the Maggid was with the Baal Shem Tov, the latter would reveal spiritual insights. If the Maggid were to leave, the flow of the Baal Shem Tov's "spring" would lessen."
[2] *Lev Sameach,Bereishis,*p. 6

RABBI Yaakov Yosef of Polonnoye,[1] the author of Toldos Yaakov Yosef, was at first vehemently opposed to the path of the Baal Shem Tov. Eventually, however, he attached himself to the Baal Shem Tov with great love and awe. Though there are many versions of how this came about, the author of Shivchei Habesht[2] relates an account that he heard directly from Rabbi Yaakov Yosef.

The first time that Rabbi Yaakov Yosef prayed in a house where the Baal Shem Tov was staying, he began to weep uncontrollably in the middle of his prayers, more than ever before. He realized that the emotions that were moving him did not originate from within himself but came about through the powerful influence of the Baal Shem Tov. From that time on, he was a devoted follower of the Baal Shem Tov.[3]

---

[1] D. 1782
[2] The first book of stories about the Baal Shem Tov. The volume was published in 1814, fifty-five years after the Baal Shem Tov's death.
[3] *Tzror HaChayim*, p. 10d

IN the city where the Baal Shem Tov lived, a brilliant Talmud Chochum[1] was so opposed to the "new" way that he refused to listen to the teachings of the Baal Shem Tov, and did not believe in his purported spiritual power. Nevertheless, the Baal Shem Tov dearly wanted him to be his disciple.

Once, this Talmud Chochum encountered a very complex Torah law, and a certain Tosephos[2] that he could not understand. And though he devoted a great amount of mental energy to trying to understand it, he was unsuccessful. This troubled him greatly.

One night, in a dream, he saw himself being lifted up to the supernal worlds. He was taken into ever more concealed chambers, each filled with greater spiritual illumination than the one before until it was so bright that he had to shut his eyes. Finally, he was brought to a very high, supernal chamber and told to look around.

---

[1] An expert in the entire Talmud and legal codes
[2] Thirteenth-century commentary on the Talmud

When he opened his eyes, he saw many great sages and Tzaddikim sitting about a table and studying Torah. The Baal Shem Tov, sitting at the head of table, said to him, "Why are you having so much trouble understanding that Tosephos? Here is the interpretation . . ."

When the Talmud Chochum awoke in the morning, he took out his Talmud and looked over the words of the Tosephos. He saw that the Baal Shem Tov's explanation was remarkably clear and that now he easily understood the Tosephos. Nevertheless, he still thought that the explanation was from an ordinary dream and did not have anything to do with the Baal Shem Tov.

When the next Shabbos arrived, he decided to attend the Third Meal[1] at the beis medrash of the Baal Shem Tov. When he walked into the beis medrash, he found it filled with his followers standing around a table. At the head

---

[1] Seudah Shelishit, held before sundown at the conclusion of Shabbos – traditionally a time when Chasidim gather together with their Rebbe to sing and hear words of Torah.

of the table sat the Baal Shem Tov speaking words of Torah. The Baal Shem Tov immediately acknowledged the arrival of the Talmud Chochum with "Good Shabbos!" Did you look over the explanation of the Tosephos that I gave you? Did you see whether what I said was true?"

From that day on, the Talmud Chochum attached himself to the Baal Shem Tov and became a great Chassid.[1]

---

[1] *Kesser Shem Tov 2*, p. 16a

IT was the final moments of the Baal Shem Tov's life.[1] His closest Chassidim were gathered around his bedside.

"My dearest friends," spoke the Baal Shem Tov in barely a whisper, "Please sing Reb Michel's[2] niggun[3] (also known as the arousement of great Heavenly mercy niggun)." And so the Chassidim began to sing the niggun over and over.

Suddenly, the Baal Shem Tov gathered all of his waning strength, sat up in his bed and said, "I hereby guarantee you and all future generations that whenever someone sings this niggun with the intent of arousing themselves to doing teshuvah,[4] no matter where or who they are, I will hear this niggun in whatever Heavenly Chamber I am found. I will join the singer in this niggun and help arouse great Heavenly mercy, channeling Divine blessings upon him."[5]

---

[1] First day of Shavuos 5520 (1760)
[2] Reb Michel of Zlotchov, a close disciple of the Baal Shem Tov
[3] A Chassidic melody, which is intended to express and stir the soul
[4] Returning to the path of G•d
[5] *Stories of the Baal Shem Tov* by Y.Y. Klapholtz

PART IV

THE TEACHINGS OF THE

BAAL SHEM TOV

FROM the year 1575,[1] until G•d sent us the holy holy soul of the Baal Shem Tov, many Jewish scholars were, for the most part, divided between those that considered the study of Kabbalah a necessity and those that challenged its study as being spiritually dangerous. Even those who did study this esoteric wisdom were often unable to comprehend its abstract concepts and fell into anthropomorphism,[2] G•d forbid. The Baal Shem Tov taught us how to understand these concepts and how to develop a pure and whole-hearted service of G•d based upon the wisdom of the Kabbalah. He was able to clothe the details of this wisdom in the intellectual faculties of the Divine soul.

The Baal Shem Tov's teachings of Kabbalah were recorded and spread by his closest disciples within the inner circle, called the Chevreyah Kadisha. These disciples directed

---

[1] 1575 was three years after the Arizal left this world and the beginning of the spreading of his teachings.

[2] That is, they began to imagine that the spiritual concepts found in Kabbalah, many of which are explained in images drawn from human physiology, were actually describing the physical proportions of G•d who is beyond form.

their words specifically to those who toil in the holy wisdom of Kabbalah in order to deepen their understanding of their service of G•d.[1]

[1] Notes on the *sefer Sur M'Ra*

RABBI Yaakov Tzemach, a renowned Kabbalist,[1] wrote that the revelation of the soul of the Arizal was absolutely necessary for that generation. The Arizal revealed the wisdom of Kabbalah and provided that spiritually impoverished generation with a shield and a shelter to serve our Father in Heaven.

So too, the great soul of our holy Rabbi, the Baal Shem Tov, was truly Heaven-sent. He descended from the highest of spiritual worlds to become revealed in our time, this generation before Moshiach, in order to illuminate the world and its inhabitants with the Divine light of the holy Torah.

It is true that in previous generations, there were many individuals who served G•d with all their heart and soul, toiling in the Torah day and night. However, they were only able to accomplish this in one of two ways. Either they were blessed by G•d with prosperity, which allowed them to set aside

---

[1] Approximately 1610–1665

time for Torah study and prayer. Or, they turned their backs on the cares of this world and accepted poverty with love in order to toil over Torah. Everyone else however — the poor who could only make a living with great effort, whether at home, in the fields, in the markets, or in the streets — could not feel the Divine light of G•d in their Torah study and prayer. Indeed, they were very far from it.

Furthermore, even among those people who could set aside a significant amount of time for Torah study, there were few who were wise enough to be able to find protection in the Torah from the yetzer harah,[1] the great enemy that lurks in the heart of man.

Fortunately, G•d took compassion on us in this spiritually impoverished generation, when everyone is pressed to make a living, when no one has money and everything is expensive, when there are fewer and fewer diligent students of Torah each day, and when no one

---

[1] Evil inclination

searches for G•d. He sent us an angel-like being from heaven to enliven us — our holy rabbi, the light of Israel, the Baal Shem Tov. The Baal Shem Tov enlightened us so that even in the most difficult times, we can still remember G•d and His Torah and be able to separate the evil from the good in everything we do, in our actions and our words.

Still, if we look at ourselves truthfully, we see a complete lack of humility. Our attitudes come from the evil inclination that has accompanied us since birth and blinds us to the truth. The evil inclination makes us think that we are humble, although we are only becoming prouder. For if we were truly humble, we would become angry and belittle the yetzer harah. We would consider it inappropriate to listen at all to the yetzer harah. Perhaps we might even learn something from the words of the Baal Shem Tov — perhaps we might even believe, without any doubt, that his words were sent from Heaven.

Now, though, we must thank G•d for sending us in His great love and compassion, an angel and redeemer to enlighten our eyes in the way of Chassidism. For every Jew can follow this path, strengthening themselves to fear G•d even amidst suffering, hardship, and poverty. The goodness that one derives from even a little Torah study and the performance of mitzvos will cause a great amount of Divine light to flow through us and prevent us from following after our eyes and heart.

The Baal Shem Tov taught that even when you are preoccupied by daily activities and business, you can still follow the words of our holy Torah: "You shall not steal money; neither shall you deal falsely, nor lie to one another."[1] Likewise, you will be just in your measurements: "a just ephah and a just hin,"[2] because this is G•d's will as expressed in His Torah.

---

[1] Leviticus 19:11
[2] Leviticus 19:36

Therefore, by following the Baal Shem Tov's teachings, you are always serving G•d, even when you are involved in business or walking through the market the same as if you were actually studying Torah. This is even truer if one knows the secret of how to make unifications.[1] Then, you can make unifications even with mundane things, as the Baal Shem Tov taught us, to the extent that one is actually considered to be studying the secrets of Torah and the writings of the Arizal, when involved in business, walking through the marketplace, or in conversation with people. Thus, G•d clothes Himself in our physical desires, in order to allow us the opportunity to elevate these very desires and transform them into a desire for Him. However, if we cannot find G•d there, and come close to sinning, G•d lowers Himself even more, to clothe Himself in the very force that

---

[1] Connecting the spiritual essence of the physical world with its spiritual source

now keeps us from carrying out the act of sinning.[1]

∞

---

[1] *Imrei Noam*

"WHOEVER fulfills a mitzvah[1] is rewarded, and his life is lengthened."[2]

Regarding this statement, the Baal Shem Tov taught:

We can deduce this from the fact that G•d Himself conveyed only a single positive commandment directly – "I am G•d, your L•rd" – the first of the Ten Commandments,[3] which was to teach us that even properly fulfilling one single commandment is sufficient.

Furthermore, as I[4] heard from my teacher the Baal Shem Tov, we can also prove this by logical deduction. The earlier sages said that it is possible to grasp the secret of G•d's Unified Oneness by holding on to any "part" of that Oneness, because that is the same as holding on to the entirety of the Oneness. Hence, since the

---

[1] Divine Commandment
[2] Tractate Kiddushin 39b
[3] Tractate Makkoth 24a, where it says that the second commandment forbidding idolatry was also conveyed directly by G•d. The Baal Shem Tov, however, is only referring here to positive commandments, and not to negative prohibitions.
[4] Rabbi Yaakov Yitzchak Pollonoye

Torah and the Mitzvos[1] emanate from G•d's essence, from His True Oneness, when one fulfills one Mitzvah with the proper intentions and devotions, one is grasping a "part" of the Oneness.[2]

---

[1] Divine Commandments
[2] *Keser Shem Tov* II 02

"**SOMETIMES,** violation of Torah is its observance. We learn this from G•d's telling Moses after the breaking of the Tablets, 'That you broke,'[1] which implies approval for his having broken them."[2]

The Baal Shem Tov taught the following on this teaching from the Talmud.

How can violating the Torah possibly enhance its observance? When one eats, drinks, or is otherwise involved in mundane affairs, they are "violating" the Torah because of not studying it or explicitly serving G•d at that time. However, at this time, their soul has a chance to rest from its enthusiasm to serve G•d and gather new strength to return to an even higher level of closeness to G•d. This spiritual phenomenon is alluded to in the verse, "The chayos (angels) run to and fro;"[3] this is why

---

[1] Exodus 34:1
[2] Tractate Menachoth 99b
[3] Ezekiel 1:14

"violating" the Torah sometimes is its observance.[1] [2]

∞

---

[1] Toldot Yaakov Yoseph, Tazria 2; Devarim 2. There are two reasons why this must be so. First, if one were not to periodically "cool down" from intense spiritual experiences, one might reach a stage where one's soul would become so united with G•d that it would completely lose its separateness. At that point it would not be able to return to the physical body. The other reason is because perpetual pleasure loses its glamour and becomes boredom. Thus, if one were constantly experiencing peak spiritual pleasures, they would no longer be considered pleasurable experiences. Regarding why one then rises to even more intense experiences, this is because the anguish of separation intensifies the pleasure of return.

[2] *Keser Shem Tov* II 02

A man once journeyed to the Baal Shem Tov with a question. He had studied the natural sciences and philosophy and had discovered that according to the laws of nature, the sea was supposed to split at the very moment of the Children of Israel's arrival there. Why then, he wondered, do we believe that the splitting of the sea was such a miraculous event? This question troubled him deeply.

When he arrived at the beis medrash of the Baal Shem Tov, even before he had asked his question, the Baal Shem Tov summoned all the townspeople to hear a sermon.

"There are fools and heretics in this world who have trouble believing that the splitting of the sea was a miracle," he said. "These people have eyes, but cannot see.

It is written: 'In the beginning, G•d created the heavens and the earth.' The name of G•d, 'Elokim'[1] has the same gematria[1] as of

---

[1] Each of G•d's Names has a different significance. The Name used in the first chapter of Genesis, describing the creation of the world, is Elokim.

'Hatevah,'[2] for nature is also created by G•d. Thus, the Sages said on the verse, 'And the sea returned to its strength,'[3] that 'G•d made a condition with the sea.'[4] From the very beginning, G•d had built it into the sea to split before the Children of Israel at that time. This in fact, makes the miracle even greater! From the beginning of creation, G•d created the natural order for the sake of the Children of Israel, as it says: 'In the beginning' — for the sake of Israel, who is called 'the beginning.'[5] This nature of the sea was created for Israel. Had they not required this miracle, G•d would not have built it into the sea."[6]

---

[1] Numerology on the basis of numerical equivalents for each letter of the Hebrew alphabet.
[2] Both "Elokim" and "Hatevah" (the Hebrew word for nature) are numerically equivalent to 86.
[3] Exodus 14:27
[4] Midrash Rabbah, Bereishis 21:6. The words "to its strength"—l'eitano—is interpreted by the Sages as l'tanao— "to its stipulation." That is, G•d made a stipulation with the sea when He created it, that it would split at that very moment for the Children of Israel.
[5] See Rashi's commentary on Genesis 1:1. Israel is called "the beginning," as in the verse, "Israel is the L•rd's hallowed portion, the beginning of His produce." (Jeremiah 2:3)
[6] *Beis Yaakov*, Bereishis and Beshalach

THERE was a discussion among the Baal Shem Tov's closest students regarding two verses in Scripture. Of Noah it is written: "These are the chronicles of Noah. Noah was a righteous man, faultless in his generation; Noah walked with G•d."[1] Of Abraham it is written: "G•d, before whom I walked."[2] It seems that Noah needed G•d's help and support, but Abraham strengthened himself and walked in his own righteousness.

One of the Baal Shem Tov's disciples asked, "Why is it that there are times when a person clings to G•d and knows in his soul that he is close to Him, But then suddenly loses his devekus and becomes distant from the Creator?"

The Baal Shem Tov answered with the following parable. When a father wants to teach his infant son to walk, what does he do? He stands his son between his outstretched arms so that the child walks between his father's arms

---

[1] Bereishis 6:9
[2] Bereshis 24:40

and does not fall. When he comes close to his father, the father backs up slightly so that the child can approach him again. In this way, the child learns to walk. If the father didn't keep moving back, the child would only walk that short distance from where his father had first put him to where his father now stands. However, because the father moves back, the child walks further.

This is how G•d relates to His creatures. When a person is aflame with spiritual attachment, G•d must distance Himself, for if not, his devekus would be neither strong nor consistent. However, because G•d keeps moving away, the person must continually renew and strengthen his devekus. This is what King David alluded to when he said: "He will lead us eternally."[1] On this Rashi explains: "Like a man leads his small son slowly."[2]

For this reason, G•d is called "the hidden G•d." For even a Tzaddik never feels that he has

---

[1] Psalms 48:15
[2] Turei Zahav, Rosh Hashanah

reached perfection in serving G•d but always feels far from Him. This is designed so that he comes ever closer. It is the meaning of "He will lead us eternally." G•d is called "He" when He is hidden.[2] This is in order that "He will lead us eternally (al'mus) — like a child (al'miah,)[1] so that we keep coming closer.

---

[1] In both Aramaic and Hebrew, the word "elem" means "youth."

ON the verses, "Then G•d said to Moses: 'Look, I am going to rain down for you bread from Heaven. Every day, the people will go out and gather enough for each day,"[1] the Baal Shem Tov taught:

A poor person has the privilege of speaking to the Holy One every day. A rich person, however, receives all his sustenance from G•d at once, and doesn't need to ask Him for his daily needs - unless he is very righteous, and realizes that everything he owns is worthless without G•d giving it life-force.

A poor person with nothing to eat must beseech G•d each day. Thus, he merits speaking to Him every day. Furthermore, G•d must also remember the poor person daily, to provide for his livelihood. However, G•d does not need to remember a rich person each day, for He already gave him all of his needs at one time.[2]

---

[1] Shemos 16:4
[2] *Rav Yebi*, Tehilim

OUR master the Baal Shem Tov said to his disciple, the Rabbi of Kalamaya, "I love the Jew who is the least significant in your eyes, more than you love your only son."[1]

---

[1] *Leket Imrei Peninim*, p. 208b Heichal Habrocho Rebbe of Komarnoh

I[1] heard from my master, the Baal Shem Tov, that "belief" means the mystical attachment of the soul to the Holy One, blessed be He.[2]

---

[1] Yaakov Yoseph of Pollonoye
[2] *Toldos Yaakov Yosef, Ki Tavo*

PART V

THE BAAL SHEM TOV

ON PRAYER

THE Baal Shem Tov taught:

Be very careful what you say in the morning before praying. Our Sages were strict even regarding the use of permissible words, such as greeting someone before prayer,[1] because such an action can cause a blemish.

It is known that the world was created with thought, speech, and action.

The first level of creation is thought. Speech is an result of thought, and action a result of speech. When a person rises each morning, they are also a new creation, as the verse says, "They are new every morning."[2] If the person's first words are mundane, and all the more so, if they are forbidden,[3] everything said later in the day will be influenced by these first words — even their prayers and Torah studies.

---

[1] Berachos 14a
[2] Lamentations 3:23
[3] Forbidden words are profanity, gossip, or slander, among others.

This is similar to the teaching of the Zohar[1] and of the Arizal on the obligation of siblings to honor the firstborn brother.[2] The fatrher's spirit resides more in the oldest son than the other sons who obtain their father's spirit from the oldest son. Due to this spirit residing more in the oldest son, they are obligated to honor him as they are obligated to honor their father.

The firstborn takes the main portion, whereas all the other siblings are as offshoots from him. Similarly, one must be very careful to sanctify and purify the first words and thoughts of the day, and attach them to holiness. Then, all subsequent words will follow their character. And when one starts to pray, amidst the joy of having fulfilled the mitzvah of sanctifying

---

[1] Zohar 3:83a
[2] The Arizal writes that just as children are obligated to respect their parents, so must they respect their firstborn sibling. For the firstborn represents the initial creative act of the parents, from which all subsequent births draw their vitality. Thus, Jacob said about Reuben, "Reuben, you are my firstborn, my might, and the beginning of my strength. . . ." (Genesis 49:3)

speech and thought, the spoken words of his prayer will surely be answered.[1]

[1] *Sipurei Baal Shem Tov.*

THE Baal Shem Tov was once asked by his students, "Why is it that although we study Torah, pray and perform mitzvos and good deeds, our prayers remain Above, while your prayers and words are heard in Heaven, for we see that your supplications bear fruit."

The Baal Shem Tov answered them with the following parable.

There was a king's son who became lost, and found himself in a field of grazing flocks of sheep. He was very hungry, thirsty, and tired. A shepherd found him and invited him to his home. But the poor shepherd didn't have anything to graciously host a person of royalty. So he took his cleanest and best piece of cloth and spread it on the table as a tablecloth. Then he spread a clean, white blanket on the ground for the prince to lay upon and sleep. The poor shepherd had nothing else with which to honor the prince, neither bread to put on the tablecloth, nor a pillow to put on the blanket. But what he could do, he did with great honor and courtesy.

Later, when the prince returned to his father's palace home, he summoned the shepherd before him, and exalted him before all the noblemen in his Court. The noblemen then asked the prince, "Why do you exalt this shepherd so much? We always do your will in whatever you ask us."

The prince answered, "All the honor and prestige that I bestow upon the shepherd is only because he provided me in my time a need all that he possibly could, a clean tablecloth and a clean white blanket on the ground."

This is what the Baal Shem Tov said. Understand these words, for they are very profound.[1]

---

[1] *Shoshana l'Dovid*, Tehilim 2

THE Baal Shem Tov instructed his disciples to learn a passage of Zohar before each of the daily prayer services.[1] [2]

---

[1] Shacharis, Mincha and Maariv
[2] *Likutey Torah*, hadracha 7

THE Baal Shem Tov taught his students to bring themselves to a state of awe by meditating on the greatness of G•d before prayer.

"When you want to pray, first bring yourself to a state of awe,[1] for this is the gate to enter before the Blessed One.[2] Say in your heart: 'To Whom do I want to attach myself? To Him Who created all the worlds with His words, and Who enlivens and sustains them!' You should meditate on His greatness and exaltedness; then you can enter the supernal worlds."[3]

---

[1] Reverance of G•d
[2] See Shabbat 31b.
[3] *Tzava'as HaRivash*, 66

RABBI Nachman of Breslov[1] said that descendants of the Baal Shem Tov are particularly accustomed to crying out to G•d at all times. This is because they are descendants of King David whose whole life was devoted to constantly breaking his heart before G•d. This is the essence of the Book of Psalms.[2]

---

[1] A great-grandson of the Baal Shem Tov (1772–1811)
[2] *Likutey Moharan* II:1100

THE holy Rabbi Tzvi Hirsch of Kaidanov said that the essence of the path of the Baal Shem Tov is to learn how to draw upon oneself the type of worship that will be practiced in the time of Moshiach. From the time of the Baal Shem Tov onward, sparks of Moshiach's soul were manifest in the leaders of each generation. This is as the Talmud says: "Two thousand years of the days of Moshiach."[1] "Alaphim," or thousands, has the meaning of teaching, as in, "And I will teach you wisdom (ve'a'alephcha chochmah)."[2]

Each individual should teach themselves the path of devotion that will be practiced in the days of Moshiach.[3]

---

[1] Sanhedrin 97a: "The world will exist for six thousand years: Two thousand years of desolation (i.e., without Torah), two thousand years of Torah, and two thousand years of the days of Moshiach (i.e., in readiness for the Messiah)."
[2] Job 33:33
[3] *Zecher Tzaddik*, p. 10a

THE Baal Shem Tov taught:

There is a principle through which a person can know if his prayers have been answered: That is, if his heart is joyful after he prays. Just the reverse is the case if he feels depressed after completing his prayers.

Based on this, I heard an explanation of the Talmud's statement, "One day, Rabbi Buna joined Redemption to the Amidah and a smile did not leave his face the whole day." The question as to what is unusual about the way he prayed is famous.[1]

Surely he joined Redemption to the Amidah every day. He never knew, however, whether it had any effect Above. On the day that he joined Redemption to Amidah and did not

---

[1] Berachos 9b. The simple meaning of this is that he recited the blessing, "Redeemer of Israel" (go'al Yisrael) directly before the Amidah prayer. However, since the contiguity of these prayers is a normal part of the daily morning liturgy, the Talmudic commentators have sought alternative ways to understand this statement. Tosephos, loc. cit., writes that Rabbi Buna joined these two prayers together at dawn. He finished the blessing "Redeemer of Israel," and started the Amidah prayer at the exact moment of sunrise. This is known as praying like the vaskin. The Baal Shem Tov offers a different explanation.

stop smiling, he realized that he had caused a Supernal Unification.

Thus his heart was overjoyed.[1]

[1] *Toldos Yaakov Yosef*, Ekev

AND then there was the time, on the eve of Yom Kippur, that the gabboim[1] of the Baal Shem Tov's synagogue wanted to prohibit the poor people from sitting with their begging bowls in the synagogue because the noise disturbed the prayers. The Baal Shem Tov told the gabboim not to stop the beggars. He related that once, the kelipos[2] joined forces to overcome the side of holiness. But because of the rattling of the coins in the begging bowls on the eve of Yom Kippur, they were completely dispersed.[3]

[1] Sextants
[2] Impure spiritual forces
[3] *Midrash Pinchas HaChadash* 55

THE Baal Shem Tov gave the following parable.

"Once, the king of beasts, the lion, became enraged with his subjects. They gathered together to decide how to appease him. The fox said that he would represent them before the lion, since he knew three hundred parables with which to appease him. As they journeyed to see the lion, the fox kept saying that he had just forgotten a few more of the parables. By the time they reached the lion, he said that he had forgotten everything. Therefore, he said, each one should approach the king and appease him to the best of his abilities."

The fox's intention from the beginning, though, was only that they all follow him and surrender to the king.

Similarly, the Baal Shem Tov urged people not to rely on the prayers of the cantor on the Days of Awe, but that each individual should pray for themself.[1]

---

[1] *Ma'or Va'Shemesh*: Shemini

REGARDING praying for G•d's sake, the Baal Shem Tov taught:

Prayers for physical needs, such as: "Heal us and we shall be healed," "Bless us with a good year," etc.,[1] are like turning to a father who longs to fulfill his son's desires, and to make sure that he lacks nothing, even foolish things. For it is the nature of one who is good to do good.

G•d's only thought is how to bestow material goodness on the Congregation of Israel, who are called His children. Prayer draws down sustenance and shefa[2] into all the worlds, even into the material worlds, to satisfy G•d's longing. Thus, prayers on behalf of G•d are accepted immediately. For Heaven scrutinizes the prayers you pray for yourself, to see if they are worthy of being received. But when you pray for G•d's sake, there is nothing to stop them.[3]

---

[1] From the Amidah
[2] The flow of Divine life force into creation
[3] *Kedushas Levi*, Likutim Shonim, p. 509

I heard in the name of the Baal Shem Tov that the prayers from a person's intellect without feeling, do not physically ascend like smoke leaving the mouth. Rather, it is when a person's desires and intentions are with feeling and enthusiasm that the prayers will ascend.[1]

---

[1] *Ohr HaMeir*, Shir ha-Shirim

THE Baal Shem Tov taught:

Joyous prayer is certainly more pleasing to G•d than depressed and tearful prayers.

For example, a poor man who entreats the king with great sobs and cries will still only receive a little. However, when a minister joyfully praises the king before him and then makes his request, the king will bestow upon him bountifully, as befits the minister's stature.[1]

---

[1] *Tzava'as HaRivash,* 107

PART VI

THE MISSION OF THE
BAAL SHEM TOV

THE author of Kitzos HaChoshen,[1] once asked the holy Rabbi Tzvi Hirsch of Zidichov:[2] "What is the difference between one day and another? From the day the Baal Shem Tov became known, the number of Chasidim who follow him has multiplied. As we know, the Baal Shem Tov based himself upon the roots and foundations of the teachings of the Arizal. Yet, we don't find that any large groups attached themselves to the Arizal. What did the Baal Shem Tov innovate in the roots of Chassidus that attracts such a large following, with groups in every city?"

Reb Tzvi Hirsch answered him with the following parable.

Once, the citizens of a certain country had to appoint a king. They heard that in a very distant land, there was remarkable man: a man of towering stature and wisdom, beautiful to look upon, with flowing hair, pure as wool. He

---

[1] Rabbi Aryeh Leib HaCohane Heller (1745-1813)
[2] d. 1831

was complete with every good virtue, and there was no other as fit as he for the kingship.

However, because he was so far away, it was impossible for them to get a detailed picture of each of his merits, though they did have an overall image of his wondrous virtues. Many of the townspeople could simply not grasp or comprehend the essence of this man.

Then, someone who had traveled to that distant land and had seen that man with his own eyes, came to them and was able to describe him in every detail. His words entered the hearts of a number of the people, who could understand him. However, the majority of the people still could not understand everything based upon the traveler's testimony alone.

Finally, one wise man traveled to the distant land and actually brought the man back and set him before them, so that all who desired could see him. Multitudes flocked to him and saw his wondrous virtues for themselves. Now that they had seen what he was and they understood that he was fit to be king, they devoted themselves to him in love and set the crown of monarchy on his head.

The parable can be understood as follows:

Rabbi Shimon bar Yochai and his companions were the first to reveal a little of "G•d's secrets to those who fear Him"[1] in the Holy Zohar and especially in the two Idras.[2] However, they carefully hid the meaning of their words in the Zohar. And so it remained, until the "World of Repair" was revealed in the generation of the Arizal.

The Arizal came to make known and explain that which Rabbi Shimon bar Yochai and his companions had concealed. However, all the holy words of the Arizal deal with supernal lights and supernal worlds, and cannot be grasped by every person. Since all of his teachings related to spiritual matters in the highest heavens, the vast majority of people cannot be enlightened by them.

---

[1] Psalms 25:14
[2] Idra Rabbah and Idra Zutra; two parts of the Zohar

Finally, the holy Baal Shem Tov, revealed Divinity even in this lowly world, in each and every detail, and especially, in human beings. He showed how everything, even every limb and gesture of a person, is a garment for the Divine power hidden within it.

And he revealed the great power of Tzaddikim, who liken the form to its Creator.[1] For there is no movement or word that does not contain awesome and wondrous unifications. Every person is created upon this earth in order to achieve greatness and wonders, and to act in this world while remaining connected to the supernal worlds.[2]

---

[1] In other words, who see within the forms of creations, and especially the human form, a reflection of supernal realities, as the verse says, "From my flesh, I will behold G•d." (Job 19:26)

[2] *Divrei Tzaddikim*

THE Baal Shem Tov taught us how to bind ourselves to G•d with every action — even in mundane conversation. As it says: "'And their leaves shall not wither'[1] – this refers to the common talk of Torah scholars."[2] Thus, he brought the king before our eyes – the King of Kings, the Holy One, blessed be He.[3]

---

[1] Psalms 1:3
[2] Sukkah 21b
[3] *Divrei Tzaddikim*

THE Baal Shem Tov taught:

When a person carries with him pearls and gems, he may be attacked by robbers. Not so, however, when he carries straw. Likewise, in every generation, wicked people and a "mixed multitude" rise up against the Congregation of Israel because the latter have whatever exists in the realm of holiness.

The Baal Shem Tov saw this trouble in the last generation and cried out over it. For because of these "thorns," and their strange and distorted ways, he was unable to fix the souls of the Children of Israel by means of Torah study and Divine service.

Indeed, every Tzaddik and Chassid has an opposing force, which draws to itself all the rejected souls. At times, the wicked are able to overcome the Tzaddik.[1]

---

[1] *Notzer Chesed*, chap. 2:4F

THROUGHOUT the generations, the main work of Tzaddikim such as Rabbi Shimon bar Yochai, the Arizal, and the Baal Shem Tov and his disciples, was to bind the souls of the Jewish people to their spiritual roots, and to remove the partitions and physical desires that separated them from G•d. In this way, their souls would become bound to their spiritual roots to such an extent that they would not become detached. If this were accomplished, the Jewish people would fear G•d, even in private, and not transgress His will, even to the slightest degree.

The Tzaddikim bind their souls to G•d and the light of the Infinite by stripping themselves of their physicality and completely transcending their corporeality. At these times, they also lift up the souls of the Jewish people and bind them to their roots.

However, as the Baal Shem Tov taught, when the Tzaddikim attached their own souls to their supernal root, they had to be careful not to nullify their own existence. Otherwise, they would not be able to return to their physicality. Therefore, they had to remain attached to G•d in such a way, that even when they were busy with physical and mundane activities, their thoughts were not separate from the Creator. Thus, even when they were involved in the material world, their intention was to serve G•d. This is known as serving G•d in the aspect of smallness.[1]

---

[1] *Ma'or VaShemesh*, Pinchas

THE holy Reb Mordechai of Chernobyl[1] said, "I believe that until the coming of Moshiach — soon in our days — whenever a Jew sighs and his heart breaks with thoughts of repentance, it comes from the spiritual power initiated by the Baal Shem Tov.[2]

---

[1] 1770—1837
[2] *Mefalos HaTzaddikim*

I heard from my teacher and father-in-law, who was the chief disciple of Rabbi Yechiel Michel of Zlotchov,[1] that once when the Baal Shem Tov was traveling on the road, he stopped at a wooded area to pray. His disciples were dumbfounded to see him hitting his head against a tree, crying and screaming. Afterward, they asked him what had happened. He explained that he had seen, with divine inspiration, that in the generations just before the coming of the Moshiach there would be a multitude of rabbis, and that they would be the very ones who would impede the redemption.[2]

---

[1] 1721—1786
[2] *Otzar Chayim*, p. 134c

ANOTHER positive trait of our Rabbi, the Baal Shem Tov, was that the Divine light of Moshiach began to shine with him — a tradition we have received from Tzaddikim.

The Baal Shem Tov himself asked Moshiach, "When are you coming Master?" Moshiach replied, "When your teachings have become well-known and revealed throughout the world, and when your well springs have spread outwards, imparting to others what I have taught you, so that they too will be able to perform contemplative unifications and ascents of the soul . . ."

Thus G•d arranged for many great Jewish sages to become the Baal Shem Tov's students in order to spread his teachings.[1]

---

[1] *Divrei Shalom*, Introduction

THE great sages, from the time of the Baal Shem Tov until the complete revelation of Moshiach, are an illumination of Moshiach, as is known.[1]

---

[1] *She'eris Yisroel*, Sha'ar Hiskashrus 4:43

JUST before the Baal Shem Tov passed away and returned to his Heavenly abode, he told his only son, Reb Hirshel Tzvi, "My son, don't be afraid to take my place. I promise you that whenever you need me, whenever you call, I'll always come to help you."

The first Shabbos after the Baal Shem Tov passed away, the Chevryah Kadisha, his inner circle of Chassidim, were waiting and expecting Reb Hershel Tzvi to expound on the Torah. But he was still mourning his father's death and felt shy and inadequate to speak. The Chassidim kept urging him, "Reb Hershele, after all, your father always spoke Torah on Shabbos."

But he kept shaking his head no. Finally, the time for the third Shabbos meal arrived and the inner circle of Chassidim were sitting together with Reb Hershele. During this time, the Baal Shem Tov always taught deep mysteries of the Torah to them, his closest followers.

The Chassidim became insistent. "Reb Hershele, your father always spoke at this time. Don't you remember when he said this and when he said that?"

"You see father," said Reb Hershele, "the Chassidim have already lost respect for me."

Just then, the Baal Shem Tov began to take form before all their eyes. Everyone froze in their seats.

"Reb Hershele," they said, "We didn't mean any disrespect to you or, G·d forbid, to insult you. We're just so used to hearing your father, the Rebbe, speak words of Torah at this time on Shabbos, that we forgot ourselves."

From that Shabbos on, Reb Hershel Tzvi wore his father's white cloak, a symbol of leadership, and expounded on the Torah.

The next Shavuos, however, exactly one year after the Baal Shem Tov had passed over to the next world, Reb Hershel Tzvi and the Chassidim were sitting together and discussing the Torah as usual.

Suddenly, Reb Hershele got up and said, "My father appeared and told me that the Shechinah[1] now now dwells in Mezritch." Then Reb Hershele removed his father's white cloak and put it onto the

---

[1] G·dly revelation

shoulders of Reb Dov Ber of Mezritch. And so, Reb Dov Ber, who later became known as the Mezritcher Maggid, assumed leadership of the Chassidic movement.[1]

---

[1] *Sipurei Chassidim*

THE holy rabbi Reb Yaakov Yisroel of Cherkas told of a trip taken by his grandfather, Reb Nochum of Chernobel and a number of his close followers to his rebbe, the Maggid of Mezritch.

When they arrived in Mezritch, they met the Maggid and his son, Reb Avraham the Malach.[1] After expressing their greetings to the Maggid and the Malach, Reb Nochum and several of the disciples went on to the local inn.

Two of the followers stayed behind with the Maggid and his son. Later, when they arrived at the inn, they described the great awe they experienced in the presence of the Maggid and the Malach. They swore that the Maggid and his son were so great that none would reach their level of holiness until Moshiach comes.

Reb Nochum told them, "It is written, 'And the sun rose, and the sun set.' One generation goes, another comes, but one such as the Baal Shem Tov will not come again until

---

[1] Hebrew for Angel

Moshiach arrives. When Moshiach does come, though, there will be a Baal Shem Tov!"

He repeated these words three times to convey the message that the Baal Shem Tov will be Moshiach.[1]

---

[1] *Maasiyos Vemaamorim Kedoshim*

ON the verses, "Then the L•rd your G•d will return your captives from exile, and He will have mercy upon you. He will gather you again from all the nations where the L•rd your G•d had dispersed you,"[1] the Baal Shem Tov taught:

Every single Jew must perfect and make ready the part of Moshiach that relates to his own soul. As it is known, the word "Adam" is an acronym for the words "Adam, David, Moshiach." Adam's size was from one end of the earth to the other, and included in it all the souls of Israel. After the sin of eating the forbidden fruit, however, his stature was diminished. Likewise, Moshiach's soul will be made up of the 600,000 souls of the Congregation of Israel, as it was before Adam's sin. Therefore, every Jew must make ready that portion of his own soul that corresponds to that of Moshiach until the entire structure of the worlds is fixed and established. Then there will

---

[1] Devarim 30:3

be a universal Unification, without end. May it be soon in our days![1]

[1] *Me'or Einayim*, Pinchas

IN a letter[1] written by the Baal Shem Tov to his brother-in-law, Rabbi Gershon of Kitov, it states: "I asked my Master and teacher[2] to go with me, for it is exceedingly dangerous to ascend to the highest of the upper worlds and since that time that I arrived at my present spiritual level, I had not ascended to such places.

I went up, level after level, until I entered the palace of Moshiach, where he studies Torah with all the Tannaim and the Tzaddikim, and with the Seven Shepherds.[3] I beheld very great joy there, but I did not know the reason for this extreme happiness.

I thought this joy was, G•d forbid, because of my demise from this world. But they told me later that I was not deceased and that they derived tremendous pleasure when I performed yichudim[4] in the physical world by means of the Torah. But as to the meaning of this great rejoicing, I still do not know.

And I asked Moshiach, 'When are you coming, my Master?'

---

[1] The Epistle
[2] Achiyah HaShiloni
[3] Adam, Seth,Methuselah,Abrama,Moses and King David
[4] Contemplative unifications

He answered me, 'By this you shall know it: Once your teachings become publicly known and revealed throughout the world; when your wellsprings have overflowed beyond, imparting to others what I have taught you and you have grasped; so that they too will be able to perform yichudim and aliyahs of the neshama[1] as you do. Then all the kelipos will perish, and and it will be a time of favor and salvation."

I was bewildered at this response. I felt great anguish because of the length of time that Moshiach implied it would take until he came.

However while I was there, I learned three segulos[2] and three Holy Names which were easy to learn and to explain to others and which would allow them to perform yichudim and aliyahs of the nashama. So I felt reassured, and I thought that perhaps, using these segulos and Holy Names, my Chavrayah,[3] might also be able to attain my spiritual level. That is, they would be able to practice ascents of the soul, and learn and understand the Supernal Mysteries as I do.

---

[1] Ascents of the soul
[2] Charm or remedy of spiritual potency
[3] Inner circle of followers

But I was not permitted and I am under oath not to reveal them during my life."[1]

---

[1] *Keser Shem Tov*

GLOSSARY

Achiyah HaShaloni — The Heavenly teacher of the Baal Shem Tov. In prior incarnations, Achiyah HaShaloni witnessed the exodus from Egypt, was a prophet during the time of King David, and taught Elijah the Prophet.

Aliyah HaNeshama — Ascent of the soul.

Amoraim — Rabbinic Sages 220 CE to 500 CE.

Arizal — acronym for Eloki Rabbi Yitzchak — the Divinely inspired Rabbi Yitzcahk Luria (1535 — 1572) — whose teachings became central for virtually all Kabbalistic thought thereafter.

Baal Shem — Rabbi that utilized the powers of Kabbalah to heal the sick, ward off Demonic spirits and predict the future.

Baal Teshuvah — One who repents and returns to belief in G•d and the observance of the Mitzvos (Divine Commandments).

Chaburah — Inner circle of followers.

Chazzan — Leader of communal prayer.

Chevraya Kadisha — Holy fellowship.

Daven — Pray.

Devekus — Cleaving to G•d.

Festivals — Rosh HaShanah, Yom Kippur, Succos, Pesach, etc.

Forefathers — Abraham, Isaac and Jacob..

Gematria — Numerology on the basis of numerical equivalents for each letter of the Hebrew alphabet.

Geonim — Title given to the heads of the Jewish academies at Sura and Pumbedita in Babylonia from the seventh century until the middle of the 11th century.

Kabbalah — The teachings and doctrines that deal with the Jewish Mystical tradition.

Kabbalas Shabbos — Prayer service at beginning of Shabbos.

Kelipos — "Husk" in Kabbalistic thought, the aspect of evil or spiritual impurity that obscures the holy and good.

Mekublim — Masters of Kabbalah.

Maariv — The evening prayer service.

Mikveh — Pool of water for spiritual immersion.

Mincha — The afternoon prayer service.

Minyan — Ten Jewish men needed for communal prayer.

Mitzvah — Divine commandment.

Moshiach — Messiah — Direct descendant of King David—King and Ruler of the Jewish people during the Messianic Age.

Prophets — 1050 BCE to 450 BCE.

Rebbe — Spiritual master and leader of a Chassidic community.

Sefer— Sacred Hebrew book.

Segulah — Charm or remedy of mystical potency.

Seudah Shlishit — The third meal, traditionally eaten on Shabbos before sunset.

Shabbos— Sabbath.

Shefa — The flow of Divine life force into creation.

Siddur — The book of daily ritual Hebrew prayers.

Tallis — Prayer shawl.

Tannaim — Jewish Sages of the Mishnah 10 CE — 220 CE.

Tehilim — Psalms.

Teshuvah — Repentance; literally turning (back to G•d).

Tikkun — Spiritual repair.

Torah — Twenty four canonized scriptures of traditional Judaism. It consists of the Five Books of Moses, the Prophets, and the Writings. The

Torah can also mean any spiritual text book or idea that is connected to traditional Judaism.

Tzaddik — Saintly, righteous individual.

Tzeddeka — Charity.

Yetzer harah — Evil inclination.

Yichudim — Contemplative unifications.

BIBLIOGRAPHY

1. THE BAAL SHEM TOV ON PERKEY AVOTH
by Rabbi Isaiah Aryeh and Rabbi Joshua Dvorkes

2. IN PRAISE OF THE BAAL SHEM TOV
Translated and edited by Dan Ben-Amos and
Jerome R. Mintz

3. THE LIFE AND SAYINGS OF THE BAAL SHEM
by Salomo Birnbaum

4. THE LEGEND OF THE BAAL-SHEM
by Martin Buber

5. TALES OF THE HASIDIM EARLY MASTERS
by Martin Buber

6. THE LIGHT AND FIRE OF THE BAAL SHEM
TOV
by Maggid Yitzhak Buxbaum

7. FROM MY FATHER'S SHABBOS TABLE
by Rabbi Yehudah Chitrik

8. BAAL SHEM TOV FAITH LOVE JOY
by Tzvi Meir Cohn

9. THE ZADDIK
by Samuel Dresner

10. THE BESHT
by Professor Emanuel Etkes

23. MIRACLE MEN

by David L. Meckler

24. CHASIDIC STORIES MADE IN HEAVEN

by Avraham Meizlish

25. THE LITTLE ZADDIK

by Louis I. Newman

26. THE SLAVE WHO SAVED THE CITY AND OTHER HASSIDIC TALES

by Harry M. Rabinowicz

27. SEEKER OF SLUMBERING SOULS

by Rabbi Zalman Ruderman

28. TZAVA'AT HARIVASH

by Rabbi Jacob Immanuel Schochet

29. RABBI ISRAEL BAAL SHEM TOV

by Rabbi Jacob Immanuel Schochet

30. THE PATH OF THE BAAL SHEM TOV

by Rabbi David Sears

31. HASIDIC TALES

by Rabbi Rami Shapiro

32. REACHES OF HEAVEN

by Isaac Beshevis Singer

33. THE STORY OF THE BAAL SHEM TOV

by Dr. J. L. Snitzer

34. A TREASURY OF CHASSIDIC TALES ON

FESTIVALS

by Rabbi Shlomo Yosef Zevin

35. A TREASURY OF CHASSIDIC TALES ON
THE TORAH

by Rabbi Shlomo Yosef Zevin

~ Dedications ~

WITH GREAT ADMIRATION AND LOVE,

WE REMEMBER OUR BELOVED

MOTHER,

GRANDMOTHER AND

GREAT GRANDMOTHER

CHAVA BAS

MENACHEM MENDEL

MENACHEM AND CHAYA FLANK

AND FAMILY

~ Dedications ~

WITH THE GREATNESS OF OUR SOULS,
WITH THE POWER OF OUR WORDS AND
ACTIONS, WITH UNCONDITIONAL LOVE WE
CAN BRING UNITY TO THE WORLD.
YET NOTHING CAN HAPPEN WITHOUT THE
ASSISTANCE OF THE CREATOR.
MIGHT WE ALL BE BLESSED
WITH HIS ETERNAL LIGHT.
SPECIAL DEDICATION TO:
ALINA SIELICKA, GERRAH SELBY,
ALFIE FITZPATRICK AND BRODIE
FITZPATRICK

~

DEDICATED TO ALL THOSE WHO
GRACIOUSLY PARTICIPATED IN THE
PUBLICATION OF DIVINE LIGHT. MAY THEY
BE SHOWERED WITH BLESSINGS OF
GOODNESS BOTH PHYSICALLY AND
SPIRITUALLY

~ Dedications ~

IN HONOR OF PUBLICIZING
THE BAAL SHEM TOV'S DIVINE INFLUENCE
THROUGHOUT THE WORLD.
DEDICATE TO SARAH RIVKAH SPIRA BY HER
LOVING PARENTS IGOR AND TATYANA SPIRA

~

IN LOVING MEMORY OF
MR. VICTOR GELB
MR. DAVID SALAMON
MRS. TOBY SALAMON BY
RUTHIE AND SAM SALAMON AND FAMILY

~

IN SINCERE GRATITUDE
RANDY AND JULIE DIAMOND

~

IN HONOR OF OUR FAMILY
LEE AND MARLA WEISBERG

~ Dedications ~

DEDICATED TO SUCCESS IN SPREADING
THE TEACHINGS OF THE BAAL SHEM TOV.
SAMUEL, ALLA, ARYEH LEIB AND CHAIM OSHER
GALPERIN

~

DEDICATED IN LOVING MEMORY OF
SENDERS AND FRANCIS KOLITCH BY
YOSEPH AND SHERILYN MANDELBAUM

~

IN LOVING MEMORY OF
LARRY AND BETTY SEFTEL
ROSALYN SIROTA
ALLEN AND CAROL SEFTEL AND FAMILY

~

IN LOVING MEMORY OF
BENYOMIN YAAKOV BEN SHMUEL HACOHANE
TZVI MEIR, BASHA, DANIEL AND AVRAHAM COHN

~ Dedications ~

IN HONOR OF YONATON WAXMAN ON THE
OCCASION OF HIS 20TH BIRTHDAY ON THE 9TH OF
ADAR. HASHEM HELP HIM GO FROM STRENGTH TO
STRENGTH IN HIS TORAH AND MITZVOS.
HIS LOVING FAMILY ORLIE, LARRY, BENJIE,
AVIGAIL, GAVRIELLA, ALBERT, AARON WAXMAN

~

IN LOVING MEMORY OF
MORDECHAI MENACHEM MENDEL BEN ELIEZER
DEVORAH BAILA AND AVROHOM SPADONE AND
FAMILY

~

IN HONOR OF DANIEL JOSEPH WELYTOK FOR HIS
ACCOMPLISHMENTS AND LOVE OF READING AND
APPRECIATION OF JUDAISM
BY HIS LOVING PARENTS
JILL AND DANIEL WELYTOK

~

~ Dedications ~

THE PATH OF THE BAAL SHEM TOV TO BRING
MOSHIACH AND CHANGE THE WORLD TO A
PEACEFUL G•DLY PLACE

~

BERNICE AND ALAN GREEN

~

THE PORTNER FAMILY

~

IN MEMORY OF ESTHER BAT LELA
BY RUBEN AND LULU MISRAHI

~

IN HONOR OF PENINA RUTH SEED
BY DAVID AND DORIT SEED

~

~Dedications~

IN LOVING MEMORY OF
ESTHER BAT RACHAMIM Z"L PESSAR

~

IN MEMORY OF MOSHE BEN CHAIM OF BLESSED
MEMORY BY HIS FAMILY

~

CONGRATULATIONS ON THE SECOND
VOLUME BY MEL AND MARCIA WAXMAN

~

IN HONOR OF OUR PARENTS
MR. AND MRS. NATHAN POLLACK

~

BEST SUCCESS JONATHAN AND RACHEL
KAPLAN AND THE UPCOMING BIRTH

~

~ Dedications ~

IN THE MEMORY OF KENNETH M. SCHWARTZ
BY ROBERT N. PELUNIS

~

MAZEL TOV, I APPRECIATE THE JOY SPREAD
BY THE BST TIMES HOWARD AMSTER

~

DEDICATED TO MIRIAM YITA BAS ZISSEL
BY CAROL AND DAVID HIRSCH

~

TO TZVI MEIR HAKOHEN, A MESSENGER OF
TRUTHS, A GATHERER OF HOLY SPARKS AND
MY FRIEND BY CARY SENDERS

~

DEDICATED IN LOVING MEMORY OF SHURA FUCHS
BY SIMON FUCHS

~

~Dedications~

IN HONOR OF THE MARRIAGE OF

YOSSI AND ELISHEVA BIALO

~

IN HONOR OF IN HONOR OF OUR CHILDREN

ROBERT, LAUREN AND YAAKOVA

BY MARK AND NANCY AEDER

~

WWW.MEZUZAH.NET

Home of the World Wide Mezuzah Campaign

The fundamental goal of The World Wide Mezuzah Campaign is to unify the Jewish people. By fulfilling the mitzvah of Mezuzah, this unity can be accomplished by each Jewish person: man, woman or child. The mitzvah can be easily fulfilled by affixing a kosher Mezuzah on the "Doorpost of Your House or upon Your Gates," as required by Jewish law.

The World Wide Mezuzah Campaign.
A project of the Baal Shem Tov Foundation
a 501(c)(3), non-profit organization
www.baalshemtov.com

BAAL SHEM TOV TIMES

Spreading the Divine light of the legendary
Kabbalah Master and Mystic

Rabbi Yisrael Baal Shem Tov

-A weekly email publication-

Featured Sections:

Baal Shem Tov Story
Torah Baal Shem Tov
Heart of Prayer
Divine Light
Kesser Shem Tov

ABOUT THE AUTHOR

Tzvi Meir Cohn (Howard M. Cohn) is a Patent and Trademark Attorney (CohnPatents.com). He attended Yeshiva Hadar Hatorah in Crown Heights, Brooklyn after completing his university studies in Engineering and Law. While studying at the Yeshiva, he discovered a deep connection to the stories and teachings of the Baal Shem Tov. More recently, he founded the Baal Shem Tov Foundation which is dedicated to spreading the teachings of the Baal Shem Tov throughout the world in order to hasten the coming of Moshiach. To spread the teachings of the Baal Shem Tov, Tzvi Meir created a website, www.BaalShemTov.com and publishes a weekly newsletter, the Baal Shem Tov Times. Also, he initiated the World Wide Mezuzah Campaign (www.Mezuzah.net) as a project of the Baal Shem Tov Foundation. Tzvi Meir gives live presentations of his original music and Baal Shem Tov stories to welcoming audiences.

Made in the USA
Charleston, SC
20 September 2010